Earth Dweller

The Book of North
Earth Dweller

Forest Mother, Land Guardians,
and Bone Deep Wisdom

shunahsii rose

Rising Heron Press

Ann Arbor, MI

The Book of North - Earth Dweller
Forest Mother, Land Guardians, and Bone Deep Wisdom

Copyright © 2024 by ShuNahSii Rose

All rights reserved. Please support our community by purchasing the book. We ask that you do not reproduce any portion of this book without written permission from the author, except in the case of brief quotations. If you are Black, Indigenous, Trans, or otherwise exceptionally hit by the violence of this culture and you are in need of this medicinal writing, reach out to us. Our commitment to community care is sincere and we will do our best to put a copy of the book in your hands. For more information or permission requests contact us at the website below.

Printed in the United States

Cover and book design by ShuNahSii Rose & Maro Beauchamp

All images are copyright © ShuNahSii Rose except for image on page 103 © Elinor Freeland.

ISBN: 979-8-9872171-2-2

First Edition: December 2024

Rising Heron Press
Ann Arbor, Michigan

www.risingheronpress.org

For my Grandmother, Anja -
the rebel keeper of our old ways

A medicine booklet of writings on elemental earth.

Contents

North - Prayer of Acknowledgment   15

Introduction and Core Teaching: 17
North on the Wheel

Guardians of the Forest

Guardians of the Forest:
Ancestral Archetypal Inheritance

Jaga - Forest Mother   27

Forest Mother and Sacred Actvism   51

The Antlered One   63

Grandfather   64

Guardians of the Forest: Trees

The Web of Relations and Learning to Listen 73

Eyes of the Forest - Mothers and Protectors 81

Ritual Blessings

Door Washing and Salt at the Threshold 91

References and Resources 97

North

North

North welcomes us into the black night of dreaming
trust
reformulation only possible
in unseen spaces

chrysalis of becoming
rites of mystery and gestation
we only arrive here
through surrender

no longer what we were
not yet what we will be
old selves give way
to feed the mycelial web

the Mother Tree
the ongoing of earth's ways
will always rise again

North

North is the great repose and reformulation. The rest that comes after life. The dreaming and restoration that follows falling asleep. In the sweeping motion of time, in the day or the season, North follows the setting sun and presides over the quietude of Winter...

the fallow field

the time of silence

North is the singing soil beneath our feet and the physical place of *here*

honoring the Spirits of the Land

North

North lives within a family of elements and directions...

North and Earth
the body - home, health, work, and earth-honoring lifeways as environmentalism

East and Air
the mind - thoughts, ideas, beliefs, and collective philosophies and belief systems

South and Fire
the spirit - instinct, actions, energy, will, and collective dance and liberation

West and Water
the heart - feelings, dreams, memories, longings, and collective music cultural arts

North corresponds to the physical realm - the wisdom of the body and our relationship with the material world. The medicine of North guides and informs us in right relationship with earth and *matter* - with what *matters*. Right relationship with the material world, moving beyond compulsive blind extraction and consumption born of loneliness and disconnect, necessitates a return to reverence and respect for the

Earth as Mother

The etymological root of matter is the same as the root of mother.

materia
"substance from which something is made"

from mater
"origin, source, mother"

North is a slowing pace and deep nourishment on a cellular level that reconnects us to the ancient knowing of the land. North is Home.

Guardians of the Forest

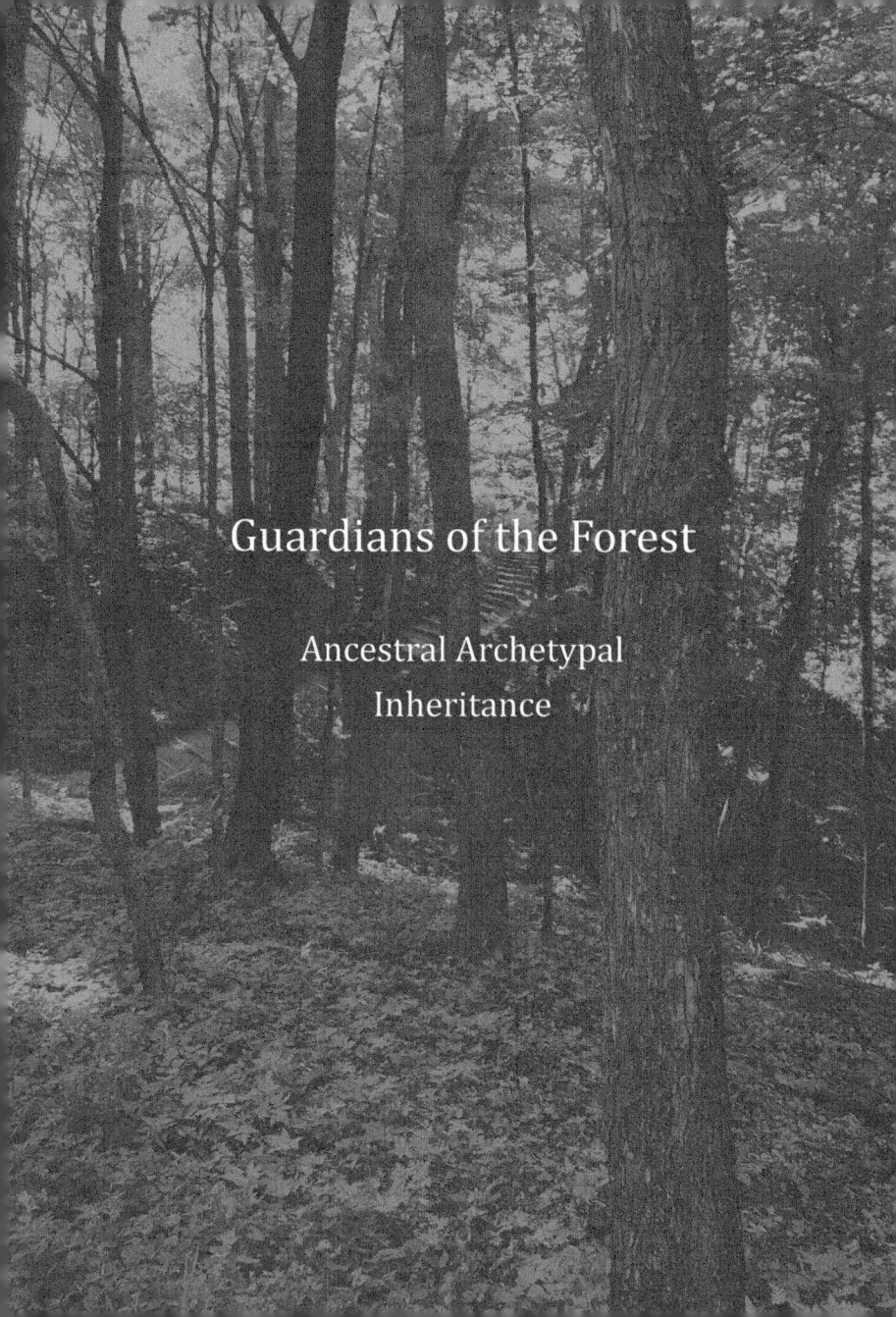

Guardians of the Forest

Ancestral Archetypal Inheritance

Jaga - Forest Mother

she is Old
preceding lines and boundaries
only frightening
to those who fear the truth

she presides over
the forest heart
cyclical time
bone deep truth
and the medicine of a good death

wild grandmother leaves no tracks
you only find her
if she lets you

At the heart of a deep, dark forest dwells a very old Grandmother who presides over many mysterious things: cyclical time, bone-deep truth, and the sanctity of the forest itself as a keeper of life's ancient rhythms. Without these knowings, whole cultures become lost to themselves and wreak havoc on the world. But to this day, she is waiting here for us. In the pulse of a quiet moment, or in our dreams, the Jaga unfurls the woven earth and brings us to remembering - the stories of mycelium carrying news throughout the land, bird tracks leaving messages in snow, and the frailty

of humans as the most likely to forget the magic that governs life on Earth. Hers is the realm of initiation and protection of what is holy - and so, of course, patriarchy hates her and tries to bury her in lies.

The stories of our oldest mothers, our guardian spirits, often come to us in shreds and tangles offering truth beneath the distortion - but we have to look and listen carefully. Finding the underlying truth asks our willingness to sit patiently - by the fire, or on the forest floor - and let them come to light. Unbinding them from lies as we venture into their realms, it is most often our bodies that will recognize the truth and return to us what's ours - the gift of right relationship laid before us in our old stories. Stories as remedy for attempted obfuscation and theft of agency. Stories as a roadmap for culture beyond extraction and built-in obsolescence. Stories as dispersers of cultural amnesia - a call back to center and our rightful place among creation. Stories as relief.

Be warned though, it takes discernment and the ability

to cut through lies to find our way to these old stories and we must come prepared. Extractive societies benefit from painting our old customs and spirits of the land as dangerous or ugly - especially if they are wild, or women, and most especially if they are old. Why are all the old women painted as evil? Because they are wisdom keepers and disruptive to a culture based on lies. We are intentionally steered away from them and their fearless, life-protecting ways are replaced by a theology of duality - breaking our stories and life on earth into parts and pieces in perpetual war with each other: good/bad, dark/light/, forgiving/discerning. A Grandmother can be both tender and forgiving *and* absolutely terrifying if you come for what she loves.

A benevolent mother, or grandmother, will bare her teeth if you approach without regard because she is also a protector. And the older she gets, the clearer she is about this, the less she has to lose. Within earth-honoring cultures, the Grandmothers and true elders in general, are keepers of our code of conduct with each other and with the earth. They remind us that

approaching with regard is a basic necessary courtesy. The ongoing of creation depends upon it. The Jaga insists on regard upon entering her forest, and in the old stories, she has the means to back it up. Intimacy with the land gives her power and many allies who also love the land and the mysteries of life and death. This is why patriarchy fears her, and why we should be suspicious of the infectious tales it tries to braid into her truths.

We learn, true of the Jaga, an ancient Slavic Grandmother god, that she dwells within a virgin forest, old growth and sovereign - quiet beyond reason. We learn also that she bestows blessings of clear sight and the way home for those who seek her rightfully. Then, jarringly, to distract us from her company, comes the story that because she is old and gray, she is terrible and untrustworthy. Simply being in her company will lay this bold lie bare.

The first thing to know about her, the Jaga or Baba Yaga, is that she is old. Older than, and presiding over, honest cyclical time itself. *She precedes the nation-state.* Our oldest archetypes and keepers of tradition, by nature, transcend and challenge constructed borders of our times - geographically, culturally, spiritually, and psychologically. Like many original mothers who precede manmade boundaries and limitations, the Jaga is a weaving of old land spirits and folk customs that defy our current maps - she lives in the old-growth forests, and the oldest Slavic tribal stories and traditions. Her stories and her kin herald from what we now know as Poland, Belarus, Ukraine, Lithuania, and Russia - under her guidance, preservation of the land is steadfast, and war is not the norm.

The entire globe was once populated with cultures, stories, and traditions that centered relationship with and reverence for the land. Many Indigenous cultures are still keeping this fire alive today against all odds. As people of the earth, our stories and customs developed over thousands of years in relationship with place to keep the people and the land healthy and intact. When we follow the threads of history, it is clear that the defiling of the forest guardians and obscuring of our stories is synonymous with the defiling of the forest and harmonious life on earth. But what is timeless is eternal and our Grandmothers persist.

The Jaga - Original Time and Liberation

Original time is cyclical and born of our connection to the seasons. It moves in a fluid spiral that allows for change and rest. All over the earth, in original cultures, each of the seasons has their corresponding traditions, ceremonies, and duties born of reverence and relationship. In earth-honoring cultures, schedules are based on these traditions and they endure for thousands of years. Our Jaga keeps this older time as is reflected in her horses and their men.

Jaga has three horses accompanied by men of a corresponding color - they ride through the forest to announce the turning of time - day in and day out this rhythm perseveres. Jaga's first horse and rider are white and herald the Dawn. Her next horse and rider are fiery red and welcome Day. Her third horse and rider are deepest black and bring the Night. Together, they mark the passing of time as it moves inside our bones - a time that we remember. As simplistic as this may sound, reclaiming natural time in the way we live our lives, is key to liberation and remains with us here in life.

My youngest daughter is a flower farmer and we happened to have a conversation about seasonal planning and the rhythm of the year as I was writing this portion of the book. I was telling her how, at this time of dwindling light, as tending the garden comes to a close, I feel a great sweeping of the year that's passed as the stage is set to dream anew. As a farmer, she agreed and noted how the quieting of external duties heralds a time to reflect - taking inventory of what you've learned in the growing season and planning for the future. To this day, even the simplest task of growing a garden reconnects us with natural time and illuminates how much gentler it is on our bodies and the earth. Interrelationship with the earth is not a metaphor and our stories are not only our inheritance but a road map to a better future in which the earth can thrive.

In our original ways, and the ways of the sentient earth, time is a spiral and death is part of an ongoing cycle. In patriarchy, time is a line with death at the end. This story is used to instill fear and to keep us from our power. Linear time, divorced from natural rhythms and broken into pieces, has us racing to the end. It instills a panic that capitalism feeds on that makes us easy to exploit and to divide. This view of time, careening toward an *end*, pressures us to chase fulfillment with consumption and accept that everything is for sale - our bodies are commodified, our psyches commodified, our families and communities, our skills and talents, and our earth commodified. We know it is not sustainable, but without the stories that expose what is beneath and return to us our legacy - the truth of cyclical time, and the beauty and comfort of interrelationship - we are bound to lose our way.

In the Motherpeace tarot deck, created in the late

1970s by feminist scholar and shamanic practitioner Vicki Noble and her collaborative partner Karen Vogel, the Devil card, archetype number fifteen (XV) in the major arcana, speaks to the nature of both personal and collective addiction - bondage in habits and routines that we know are destructive but can't manage to break free from. It pictures a pyramid culture with room for very few at the top, held up by the toil and expense of the many far below. **The ongoing of cultures of extraction relies on our acceptance of untruths** - about time and relationship, as well as power and wealth. In a cultural model of harm and extraction such as the Western model sweeping across our planet, money is seen as wealth and conquest as power, but this perspective is not inevitable and relies on the amnesia of our global earth-honoring traditions and history. In this depiction of the Devil card, atop the great pyramid of exclusion, sits a solitary white dude and a big ole' clock - it is the clock of broken time, the time clock that we punch as we check in and out of the only world we are offered if we accept this lens of separation as the truth.

Jaga and her cronies offer a different story. As a people (and a species), we need our Grandmothers - lest this tale of broken time gains the power to steal our souls. Grandmothers, by nature, stand closer to death and their reckoning can shake us awake and bring us back to center. It is not that original time has no consequence, it's that the reckoning it offers is in service to a life well lived, not to exploitation. It's true that, in Jaga's presence, we know that death is coming, but this knowledge is not to scare us. It is to help us to better cherish life - this is a gift the Jaga offers.

The Jaga - Becoming Soil - the Medicine of Death

Death is a sacred passage and every death deserves to be treated with dignity. In a culture that reveres dominance - they are not. As we pull just this one thread, the thread of death with dignity for all, it exposes the normalization of violence and all manner of sins with devastating consequences - for the people and the earth. If we engaged in an exercise in cultural reimagination and reverse-engineered what it would take to treat every single death - the death of trees, animals, insects, and all people - with dignity, it would necessitate this violent system toppling.

This brings us full circle to the concept of *regard*, a code of conduct that Jaga is so vehement about, and why she's often read as severe - especially within patriarchy. A good death demands a good life and she protects this interrelationship. *Jaga heralds from, and holds within her, a time preceding war. And war changes how we die.* It also separates us from life and changes how our deaths are handled. For example, it was not until the Civil War on the Indigenous land referred to as the United States, that the modern funerary industry was born. Up until then, the deaths and bodies of our loved ones were handled in the home - with intimacy, skill, and the regard you would extend to someone that you loved. No distance from life's passages.

From tens of thousands of years ago, we find ancestors laid lovingly in the earth - turning back to soil, their very bodies feeding life. I know these subjects are taboo, but we have to turn and face them or we leave ruin in our wake. I read an article sometime in the last year on decomposition as part of life. While I hold a firm commitment to giving credit where credit is due, please forgive me here as I cannot for the life of me find where I read it - if you recognize it, please let me know. In the story the woman tells us of her garden and how one morning she comes out to find a fallen doe. The doe had no indication of injury or stress, it seemed she had simply died there in the garden as she came to that ripe age. I should be so lucky. In any case, it got this woman thinking about the essential role of decomposition in the cycle of life on earth and this is what really struck me. We're so busy supposedly "cleaning everything up - and keeping things tidy", that we don't consider the ecological consequence of breaking the cycle of life.

Removing leaves at the end of the autumn devastates our insect population upon whom life depends. And when it comes to human bodies, with rare exception, we are either incinerating our dead, which bears a huge carbon footprint and exacerbates climate destabilization, or burying them (after their bodies are treated with toxic chemicals) in costly coffins with plastic textiles tucked into concrete within the earth. Through a lens of conscious observation, these traditions look barbaric and absurd. We are fighting earth in removing death from sight - and this is war.

The call of these old gods runs deep and relationship with them asks radical realignment. As you can see, if we take just this one of our precious and inevitable sacred passages in life on earth, and ask together, "What is wrong here?", it brings everything into question. Why are our funerary rites motivated by profit? Why do we not govern them ourselves? What is happening with our bodies in these times and what is the impact of modern customs on the earth? And maybe closest to the bone: why are so many deaths - of the elderly, of Black lives, Indigenous communities, the poor, the infirmed, immigrants hitting walls, and the rest of our kin in our family of creation - treated with such lack of regard?! Why, dear god, is there such a thing as "road kill" (of the people and the earth) in this blind race to the end?

Jaga will not settle for obfuscation - her truth takes us to the bone and that's where we need to be.

In a knowledge share with Tusha Yakovleva, a Russian ethnobotanist whose work focuses on growing reciprocal relationships between land and people, she shared an image of Baba Yaga in which her leg bone was exposed and showing through the flesh. This image struck me deeply and bears mythical significance. Why see her leg bone? What is she showing us or calling to our attention? As a keeper of core truth, bone-deep truth, Jaga makes no bones bout it - in her presence, death stares us in the face, but this isn't out of cruelty. In cultures in which death is honored as a natural part of the life cycle, looking death in the face can bear gifts of real importance - perhaps most pressing is the steadfast reminder to lead a well-lived life. Walking with death in life is also an invitation to consider how we might heal our wounded world. What if we welcomed death - of inequity, inauthenticity, blockages to care, patterns born of fear or isolation, and entire cultures based on greed?

What if the death-wielding mothers are our remedy for life?

The Jaga is a reckoning and we should welcome her again. A fear of touching death has us swallowing up life and diminishing her space with grave consequence for all the earth. We have violated holy boundaries of the land spirits and broken sacred law. She needs the forest to survive because she *is* the forest, and here's the news flash: so are we.

For me, the ancestral ways that flow in my veins are not a relic of the past. Forest Mother lives. She is my day-to-day relationship with the land that I love and the work that I do - my greatest confidante, and my wisest counsel. When all in the world feels bleak and I can't see where to turn, her voice rises on the wind and I find my way to action.

She is the foundation of my activism and the beating heart of the community that I nurture.

as long as She lives

we live

Forest Mother Speaks

open the door
let us in
we want to come

burn the purifying herbs
throw the doors and windows wide
sing
make cake
remember

we need to talk

they are coming for what is wild in you
guard it fiercely
remember

undomesticate yourself
as often as is necessary
and come outside

we are waiting for you outside
wind in your hair
your tracks in the snow
starlight pouring from the heavens

you are one of us
woven of the earth
remembering is your duty

Forest Mother's Daughter

here
I say to her
come *here*
you are welcome here

at any cost
take root in me
as I am rooted
in the earth

I will hold you
carry you
feed you
tell your stories
and defend your beauty and your honor

until I join you
in the soil

Forest Mother and Sacred Activism

Following is a 2018 excerpt from a live online journal I kept with my community during one of my periods of intensive environmental and social justice activism. This work went from 2015 to 2019 and took me to the bone. It was central to my initiation into the Grandmother years and deepened my understanding of what activism even is, or asks. As Malidoma and Sobonfu Somé (renowned teachers and tradition keepers from Burkina Faso, West Africa) always said, "It's not an initiation if you don't wonder if you're going to live through it". I wondered if I was going to live through it, and so did everyone who loved me. While there were endless hours of council and "shareholder" meetings, administrative responsibilities, phone calls, campaigns, direct actions, and brutal stress - what I am sharing here is a glimpse of the medicine that came, and the medicine I called for, in a time of deepest trial.

I made an altar
to Forest Mother
in my room —

a magical Winter
forest altar

I opened the altar
one
by lighting all of
the candles
& praying

I started hearing the land

whispering

showing me the

power of the whisper

as I walked

morning and night

The forest herself was
whispering to me
in a way
that she never had

And she was
beckoning me
to whisper back

So I did.

I whispered prayers of protection and gratitude

I whispered stories
of divine remembering

on a grand scale

of the place

we humans hold

in the tapestry of creation

our earthly family

the whispers ran
like a beautiful
clear stream
unbidden
as if granting access to a
magic
I have always carried
but never knew

The land has a power
all her own.
and while she is patient
she is not impotent
She will Rise
is rising
and we can feel this
in our Bones

We find ourselves in times with extremism on the rise and multiple crises as our earth has never known. It can be hard to not scatter in the wind - but she needs us to be present. The forest, even a single solitary tree, holds a quieting force that calls us to our senses. If we forget we are collaborting with the land, and always have been, we are already lost. How we read the story at this crossroads will have a lasting impact - let us settle into truth.

As the force of love grows stronger, the voice of fear grows louder.

But we are not alone...

the wind is waiting as our partner
as Forest Mother said
carrying blessings to future children
and songs from those long dead

carrying our inheritance
of enough to go around
if we are simply willing to remember
all of the earth is holy ground

The Antlered One

grandfather stands guard
in the quiet places
antlers wide like branches
power of the land

for millennia
my bloodlines gave him names
but he is older than my people
and older than our words

following his tracks
I find where I belong
quiet places with white pine needles
a gathering of home

Grandfather

There are so many ways that the archetypes of Earth speak to us. Sometimes it's through the long and winding trail of research and discovery. Sometimes our Grandmothers tell stories. Other times, it's simply through lived experience - direct relationship with the vibrant, breathing earth and the family that she fosters.

it was a beautiful snowy morning
where I walked most every day
by morning light and by evening dusk
I knew every inch of the way

Accompanied by my bestie, a patient golden dog, we were each doing our own thing in our respective states of awe - in deep enjoyment of this winter wonderland. Flakes were fluffy and drifting through the air like tiny clouds falling to Earth. The kind of wonder that holds your rapt attention and makes everything else fall away. Nothing more that I could want, we drifted in silent curiosity, me and the golden dog, until suddenly, we were startled by the backside of two does. Hopping up, they bolted Eastward as we surprised them nibbling rosehips. It seemed the four of us laughed together and then settled back into our grooves in that scrappy little field that has always held my heart. Then all at once, it happened - Grandfather stepped out from the woods. His antler rack imposing, he stood stock still in the falling snow.

this could be any fairytale
any story from times before
where Grandfather, the guardian
protects the secret door

Maybe 50 feet from us if that, a great and magnificent grandfather stag emerged from the forest to the West of us and stood in the path facing us. He had probably a 14-point rack and was humming with wild, yet quiet magic. Both Rio, the golden dog, and I stood silently looking at him, he looking into us, while the snow fell around us.

the old ones say stories claim us
in the meeting of our eyes
stories that mend our broken places
and give us the strength to rise

Though this was not my first up-close meeting with a buck, and it wouldn't be my last, but something about *this* moment has stayed with me for life. I was dumbstruck by the beauty of it, and of him, and after standing with many worlds alight between us for what seemed like several years, the only proper response was to bow in deepest gratitude, and then turn and give them space.

Guardians of the Forest

Trees

The Web of Relations and Learning to Listen

Hemlock, Reishi, and the Cycle of Life, Death, and Renewal

Hemlock (Tsuga Canadensis) is a conifer, with short, tender, dark green leaves, and reddish-brown bark. Though they are native to the Northeast of this continent, they are a newer tree to me. I started knowingly crossing their path about 20 years ago in a beautiful forest I hike up in Sleeping Bear Lakeshore of northwest Michigan - Aniishnaabe territory. I have a lifelong love affair with Lake Michigan and the way her presence shapes the land up there is beautifully distinct - very much like a great, dreaming mother bear. There are many species of trees in this forest, and Hemlock is a quieter tree in my experience, and a quieting tree, so it took a while before we struck up a conversation. These conversations mostly involve me sitting or standing observantly in the land of their family and just listening. Trees are often chatty, but Hemlock is a whisperer that draws you into the deepest, listening, quietude. They hold a palpable and unmistakable underlying song - a song of returning to the earth - as our bodies do in death.

You can sometimes learn about someone (like Hemlock) and ways of theirs you may have missed, by seeing them in contrast to others, The forest helps with this. Here, Hemlock shares space with Birch, and Beech, and Maple, as well as many herbaceous forest plants, but when you get to the place where Hemlock's family dwells, it feels distinct. There's compelling quietude and a deeper darkness to their home. Not in the way that Western society paints darkness as sinister or scary (fearing its own shadow, I'm sure) - more like evening falling and settling the nerves of the world. I was raised with appreciation for the

dark time of year as a time that brings us closer with our ancestors and our dreams. Traditionally, when we weren't busy trying to pretend that our lives are somehow separate from the rhythms of nature, winter and the dark time of year were welcomed for more rest, deeper dreaming, old stories, and gathering 'round. As a symbiotic host for Reishi and a tree who provides a compatible habitat for the elusive Ghost Pipe, Hemlock reminds us of invisible connections - connections that hold the world together throughout the ages. They are a keeper of timeless bonds and eternal traditions born of relationship. Sitting quietly in their presence can bring these memories back to us.

One of the things I am most fascinated with about Hemlock is their evident affinity for and bond with the Reishi mushroom. While there are many varieties of Reishi (Ganoderma) known for their medicinal value, I am speaking specifically to the most common variety that grows near me - Ganoderma Tsugae. Reishi is a glossy, reddish, polypore mushroom that grows primarily on dead Hemlock trees or parts of

Hemlock that are starting to decay. Reishi is esteemed throughout the world for their magical and medicinal potency. In traditional Chinese medicine - TCM - Reishi is known as the "Mushroom of Immortality" which speaks directly to their age-old, multi-faceted, and vast medicinal value. I am most familiar with their medicine as an immunomodulator - which means a regulator of immune response, an adaptogen - supporting the body's ability to adapt under stress, and a cardiac tonic. But the deeper you go into study, the more you can learn about the intricacies of the forest's ability to support our bodily systems and restore health and vitality.

Reishi is also known as a spirit medicine with an innate ability to support life in times of change, initiation, death, and transition. As a Mushroom of Immortality, they are quite literally the fruit that is born from the fertile decayof what has come before. Just as we are born from our ancestors - the Hemlock hosts an invisible and miraculous mycelial network within. This mycelial network draws and disseminates nourishment that produces the life/fruit of the Reishi mushroom who, in turn, has the capacity to support, stabilize, and sustain our lives as we partake of their medicine. The quietude and darkness, characteristic of the Hemlock forest, speak to us of the cyclical life stages - death, rest, and renewal - that their symbiotic medicine will support. If we listen.

Eyes of the Forest - Mothers and Protectors

Birch - Renewal and Life Awakening

In our journey with the trees in this little book, Birch follows the Hemlock and Reishi partnership. While Hemlock and Reishi are very much about the quietude and fertility that come from death and decay - Birch is about awakening new life.

There are many different varieties of Birch spanning different continents - I am speaking primarily to the white birches - Silver Birch (Betula Pendula), and Paper Birch (Betula Papyrifera) as they are the varieties I am most familiar with. The First time I remember meeting Birch was when I was a child visiting the upper peninsula of Michigan - the still very wild and beautiful land of Anishinaabe territory. I was wandering around outside and came upon some birch bark on the ground. Having never seen such a thing, I couldn't believe how much like paper it was and I was smitten. Children have a way of paying attention to wonder - they don't skip over discovery or take magic for granted the way we can as we get older. I held the "paper" in my hands and went running to my mother to show her.

It turns out, I was not the only one who noticed the Birch as a means of writing and record keeping. The Ojibwa (who are the original people of the land I was on and one of the three peoples of the Anishinaabe Three Fires alliance) used and still use birch bark scrolls to record teachings and ceremonies of the Midewiwin (their spiritual order) that helped to maintain social, spiritual, and healing practices of the tribe. Among the Indigenous people of the land I grew up loving, Birch bark is, and historically was also used to make watertight baskets for harvesting, carrying, and storing food

and water, as well as beautiful canoes for traveling the waters of the Great Lakes. Nokomis Keewaydinoquay taught me that Birch was central to the survival of the people and seen as the Grandfather (Mishomis) tree, forever intertwined in lore and importance with Grandmother (Nokomis) Cedar.

As Birches require a certain climate to thrive, they can be found at a similar longitude on more than one continent of the earth. While I was a child busy falling in love with Birch here in North America on Anishinaabe land, I had no idea that Birch was also central to my own Eastern European ancestors. In Slavic culture, these beautiful, luminous Birches are revered as protectors of the forest and the people. They feature prominently in the foods, medicines, rituals, traditions, mythology, and stories - including the story of Baba Jaga and Vasilisa in which the greening Birch heralds the youthful new life of Spring.

To both, Slavic tribal peoples, and Norse/Germanic traditions, the Birch trees are seen as feminine, watchful guardians of the forest and the people with "eyes" to help with these duties.

In the Norse/Germanic runic traditions, Beorc is associated with the Birch tree, and the goddess/archetype Dame Birch or Frau Berchta. According to Silver Ravenwolf, in her book Rune Mysteries, "Dame Birch can appear as the terrible hag of harsh purification" or the gentle mother who nurtures new growth and blesses beginnings. In the lore of the Eurasian Yakut tribes, the first shaman was nourished upon the milk of a goddess who half emerged from the cosmic birch at the "golden naval of the Earth".

In Russian folklore and tradition, Birch is also known as an original mother and protector of new life, the people, and the forest. In a knowledge share hosted by Herban Cura of NYC, Russian ethnobotanist and cultural preservationist, Tusha Yakovleva shared with us that "The Russian word for birch - beryoza (берёза) - stems from an old Slavic root meaning glowing, light, bright. It also shares a root with the verb berech (беречь), meaning to care for, to keep safe. In the spiritual lives of ancestral Slavs, Beregina, a nurturing deity, mother of all other spirits, who protects living beings and cares for growing life, is embodied in a birch tree. Beregina symbolizes spring and on her day in late spring, offerings for forest-dwelling birds and animals are placed at the bases of birches in her honor."

Medicinally, Birch is tapped for sap and either drunk as nutritive "Birch Water" or sometimes fermented into an alcoholic beverage, the tender leaves are made into skin care preparations, and the twigs are made into traditional "brooms" or "veniks" in Russian, and used to sweep the body in bath house rituals to stimulate the skin to improve circulation. From Tusha in her knowledge share "A birch vennik treatment inside the banya is regarded as a powerful healing cleanse (Pollock, 2019), said to promote blood circulation, widen the bronchial passages to increase lung health, speed up wound healing, soothe rashes, and increase skin elasticity".

Ritual Blessings

Door Washing
and Salt at the Threshold

the blessing of the threshold
with salt and light and sound
summons deep protection
as we mark the holy ground

Doorwash Ritual Blessing

While there are traditional rituals to bless doorways, passages, and thresholds in many, many cultures across the world, what I share with you here is what I learned from my Polish, working-class, badass of a Grandmother. She was my first spiritual teacher. Though she never used fancy or pretentious words, she took our spiritual hygiene seriously and taught me to do the same.

A folk ritual such as this is meant to clear, bless, and protect your home (or any other place you spend significant time in) by tending properly to the entry. My Grandmother would do this as both part of regular maintenance with the seasons, and/or in response to an acute situation - something that upset the balance in our home, building, family, or neighborhood.

Here's the thing about ingredients: they are both cultural and deeply personal. Cultures develop earth-honoring ways, including relationship with place, plants, and ceremonial traditions sometimes over thousands of years. It's very important to be sensitive and not snatch (appropriate) things that don't belong to you. As I'm sure you can imagine, it doesn't bode well for a blessing. If you know plants of your people, or are interested in researching them, tending the spiritual wellness of your home can serve as a great inspiration and motivation. And, the ingredients I've listed below are universal enough, and readily available enough, that your good intentions can be amplified without stepping on toes or traditions. And, if you need to really keep it simple, you can always just use salt water - with sincerity, it will do the job. I incorporate plants because I love them - forever - and because scent is a powerful medicine that goes a long way toward nurturing the right vibe.

A range of potential ingredients to mix into your water:

For **Cleansing and Clearing**: salt, preferably sea salt
For **Protection**: juniper, garden sage, and/or yarrow
For **Blessing and to Bring Sweetness**: rose petals and/or lavender

If you are using herbs, it's good to let them infuse for a bit. To do this, you would pop a handful of dried herbs and a ¼ cup of salt into a heatproof quart jar (or a teapot), pour boiling water over them (enough to fill the jar), cover with a lid, and let steep for at least a half hour to overnight. Shake well and then strain your mixture through a sieve into the vessel you'll work with for the ritual - it can be a bowl, another jar, or whatever you prefer.

Then, it's simple: get to washing! From top to bottom, the door frame and the door, on both sides. I like to sing while I do this as it's my favorite form of prayer. Even if you are silent, you are humbly asking that your space be cleansed, blessed, and protected as you work.

References and Resources

@adarkrainbow. "The Yaga journal: The Polish Baba Yaga." *Tumblr*, May 13, 2023, https://adarkrainbow.tumblr.com/post/717245552806576128/the-yaga-journal-the-polish-baba-yaga

Arden, Katherine. *The Bear and the Nightingale*. Del Rey, 2017.

Berger, Judith. *Herbal Rituals*. Smashwords Edition, 2014.

Brant, Beth, editor. *A Gathering of Spirit: A Collection by North American Indian Women*. Firebrand Books, 1989.

Estés, Clarissa Pinkola. *Women Who Run With the Wolves: Myths and Stories of the Wild Woman Archetype*. Ballantine Books, 1992.

Geniusz, Mary Siisip. *Plants Have so Much to Give Us, All We Have to Do Is Ask: Anishinaabe Botanical Teachings*. University of Minnesota Press, 2022.

Glinski, A. J. *Polish Fairy Tales*. Read Books Ltd, 2015.

Mayer, Marianna. *Baba Yaga and Vasilisa the Brave*. Harper Collins, 1994.

Jackson, Nigel, and Silver RavenWolf. *Rune Mysteries: Companion to the Witches Runes*. Llewellyn Publications, 1999.

Kitaiskaia, Taisia. *Ask Baba Yaga: Otherworldly Advice for Everyday Troubles*. Andrews McMeel Publ., 2017.

Kitaiskaia, Taisia. *Poetic Remedies for Troubled Times: From Ask Baba Yaga*. Andrews McMeel Publishing, 2020.

Knab, Sophie Hodorowicz. *Polish Herbs, Flowers & Folk Medicine*. Hippocrene Books, Inc, 2020.

Moerman, Daniel E. *Native American Ethnobotany*. Timber Press, 1998.

Novik, Naomi. *Spinning Silver*. Del Rey, 2019.

Peschel, Keewaydinoquay. *Puhpohwee for the People: A Narrative Account of Some Uses of Fungi Among the Anishinaabeg*. LEPS Press, 1998.

Rose, ShuNahSii. *Walking With Deer: A Live Journal of Environmental Activism*. 2018.

Sheldrake, Merlin. *Entangled Life: How Fungi Make Our Worlds*. Random House, 2021.

Starhawk. *Circle Round Raising Children in Goddess Traditions*. Random House Publishing Group, 2020.

Vogel, Karen, and Vicki Noble. *Motherpeace Tarot Guidebook*. U.S. Games Systems, Inc, 1995.

Wohlleben, Peter. *The Hidden Life of Trees: What They Feel, How They Communicate*. Greystone Books ; David Suzuki Institute, 2016.

Woodruff, Patricia Robin. *Woodruff's Guide to Slavic Deities*. R R BOWKER LLC, 2020.

References from living encounters - family, elders, and teachers:

Tusha Yakovleva - a knowledge share on Russian Folklore and Land Spirits - hosted by Herban Cura - https://www.herbancura.com/about

I want to acknowledge two Grandmothers from my life whose work and generous tutelage have influenced this body of work: my maternal Grandmother, Anja Turadek, and my spiritual adoptive Grandmother, Nokomis Keewyadinoquay - they are both now among the ancestors.

ShuNahSii Rose, born to an inner-city working-class, immigrant family of Eastern European and Irish ancestry, is an educator, author, gardener, folk herbalist, and community organizer. She has deep roots in earth-honoring traditions that trace back to her maternal grandmother and inform her dedication to liberation work.

Learn more at www.truearth.org

Made in the USA
Monee, IL
12 December 2024

73514557R00059